S0-ASU-538

CONTEMPORARY CHRISTIAN

**MELODY LINE, CHORDS AND LYRICS
FOR KEYBOARD • GUITAR • VOCAL**

HAL•LEONARD®

ISBN 0-634-06821-0

HAL•LEONARD®
CORPORATION

7777 W. BLUEMOUND RD. P.O. BOX 13819 MILWAUKEE, WI 53213

Visit Hal Leonard Online at
www.halleonard.com

Welcome to the PAPERBACK SONGS SERIES.

Do you play piano, guitar, electronic keyboard, sing or play any instrument for that matter? If so, this handy "pocket tune" book is for you.

The concise, one-line music notation consists of:

MELODY, LYRICS & CHORD SYMBOLS

Whether strumming the chords on guitar, "faking" an arrangement on piano/keyboard or singing the lyrics, these fake book style arrangements can be enjoyed at any experience level – hobbyist to professional.

The musical skills necessary to successfully use this book are minimal. If you play guitar and need some help with chords, a basic chord chart is included at the back of the book.

While playing and singing is the first thing that comes to mind when using this book, it can also serve as a compact, comprehensive reference guide.

However you choose to use this PAPERBACK SONGS SERIES book, by all means have fun!

CONTENTS

(contents continued)

ABBA
(Father)

Words and Music by REBECCA ST. JAMES,
TEDD TJORNHOM and OTTO PRICE

AFTER THE RAIN

Words and Music by CONNIE HARRINGTON,
JOE BECK and NEAL COOMER

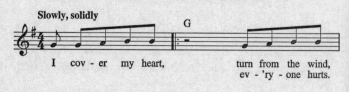

I cov-er my heart, turn from the wind,
ev-'ry-one hurts.

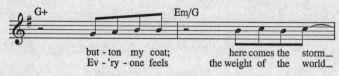

but-ton my coat; here comes the storm
Ev-'ry-one feels the weight of the world

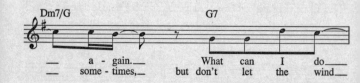

— a-gain. What can I do
— some-times, but don't let the wind

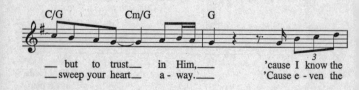

— but to trust in Him, 'cause I know the
— sweep your heart a-way. 'Cause e-ven the

deep-er my faith runs, the
rough-est wa-ters cleanse. So

G/B

strong - er I___ be - come.___ And the
when they come___ a - gain,___ let them

Eb/G

thun - der, it___ may shake___ me, but I al -
serve as a___ re - mind - er you can al -

Dm7/G   A7sus

- ways know___ that } af - ter the rain
- ways know___ that }

%S D

you can look to the sky___

Em7

___ a - gain.___ The clouds will give way___

A7sus   D/A   D   A7sus

___ to the light of the sun.___ Af - ter the rain,___

D   Em7

___ you know that you've made___ it through___ and you'll

ARISE, MY LOVE

Words and Music by
EDDIE CARSWELL

14

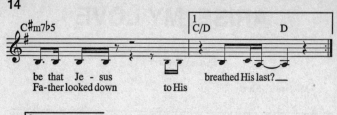

be that Je - sus breathed His last?___
Fa-ther looked down to His

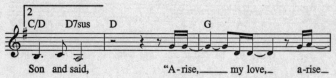

Son and said, "A - rise,___ my love,___ a-rise___

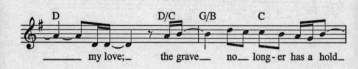

___ my love;___ the grave___ no___ long- er has a hold___

___ on___ you. No more___ death's sting, no more

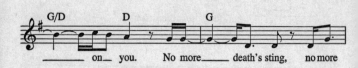

suf - fer - ing. A - rise, a -

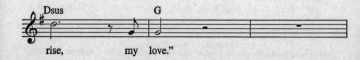

rise, my love."

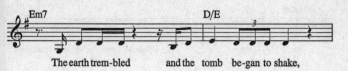

The earth trem-bled and the tomb be-gan to shake,

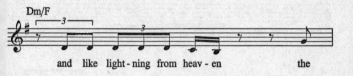

and like light-ning from heav - en the

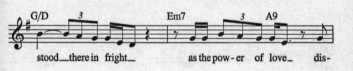

stone rolled_ a - way._ And as dead men, the guards

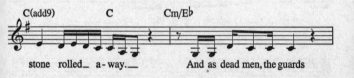

stood_there in fright_ as the pow - er of love_ dis-

played its might._ Then_ sud-den-ly a mel-o-dy filled_

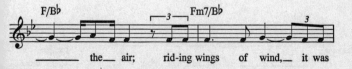

_ the_ air; rid-ing wings of wind,_ it was

ARMS OF LOVE

Words and Music by AMY GRANT,
MICHAEL W. SMITH and GARY CHAPMAN

AWESOME GOD

**Words and Music by
RICH MULLINS**

Steadily, with drive

F#m

When He rolls up His sleeve,_ He ain't just "put-tin'on the Ritz." Our
sky_ was star-less in the void_ of the night, our

Bm7   C#m7   F#m

God is an awe - some God!   There is thun-
God is an awe - some God!   He spoke in-

- der in His foot-steps and light - ning in His fist. Our
- to the dark-ness and cre - at-ed the light. Our

Bm7   C#m7   F#m

God is an awe - some God!   And the
God is an awe - some God!

Bm7

Lord was-n't jok-in' when He kicked 'em out of E-den, it
Judg-ment and wrath He poured out on Sod-om,

was-n't for no rea-son that He shed His__ blood. His re -
mer-cy and grace_ He gave us at the__ cross. I

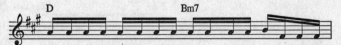

turn is ver - y close and so you bet-ter be be -liev-in' that our
hope that we have_ not_ too_ quick - ly for-got-ten that our

God is an awe - some God!}
God is an awe - some God!} Our God   is an awe-some God, He

reigns   from__   heav - en   a - bove   with

wis - dom,__ pow'r   and   love;   our

God is an awe - some_ God!   Our God   is an awe-some God, He

22

reigns   from_ heav - en a - bove   with

wis - dom,_ pow'r and love;   our

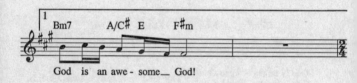

God is an awe - some_ God!

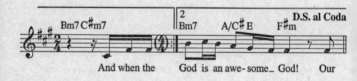

And when the   God is an awe- some_ God!   Our

CODA

God   is   an   awe - some_ God!   Our

God is an awe-some God!   Our God is an awe- some_ God!

BETWEEN YOU AND ME

Words and Music by TOBY McKEEHAN
and MARK HEIMERMANN

24

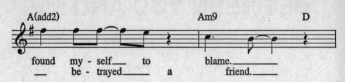

A(add2)   Am9   D

found my-self___ to   blame.___
___ be-trayed___ a   friend.___

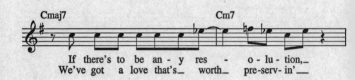

Cmaj7   Cm7

If there's to be an - y res - o - lu - tion,___
We've got a love that's___ worth___ pre-serv- in'___

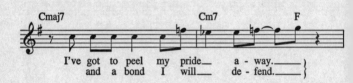

Cmaj7   Cm7   F

I've got to peel my pride___ a - way.___
and a bond I will___ de - fend.___ }

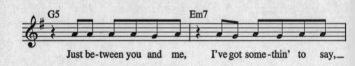

G5   Em7

Just be-tween you and me,   I've got some-thin' to   say,___

E♭maj7   F(add9)

___ wan-na get it   straight___ be-fore the sun goes down.

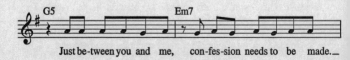

G5   Em7

Just be-tween you and me,   con-fes-sion needs to be   made.___

— Re-com-pense is my way_____ to free - dom now.

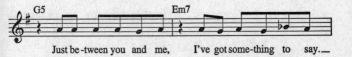

Just be-tween you and me, I've got some-thing to say.__

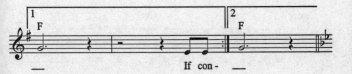

— If con - __

In my pur-suit of God, I thirst for ho - li-ness.

As I ap-proach the Son, I must con-sid - er this.

Of-fens-es un - re-solved will keep me from the throne.

Be-fore I go to Him, my wrong must be a-

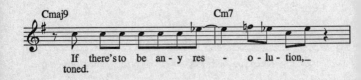

If there's to be an-y res - o-lu-tion,__
toned.

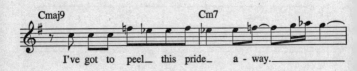

I've got to peel__ this pride__ a-way.__

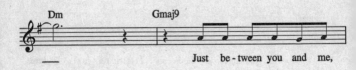

__ Just be-tween you and me,

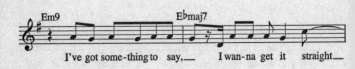

I've got some-thing to say,__ I wan-na get it straight__

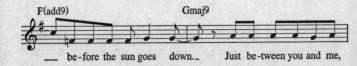

__ be-fore the sun goes down.__ Just be-tween you and me,

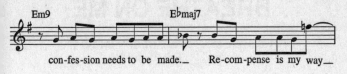

Em9   Ebmaj7

con-fes-sion needs to be made.__ Re-com-pense is my way__

Dm7   C   Gmaj9

_____ to free - dom._____ It's my way__

Em9   Ebmaj7

__ to free - dom._____

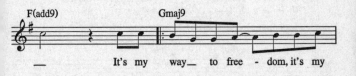

F(add9)   Gmaj9

__ It's my way__ to free - dom, it's my

Em9   Ebmaj7

way__ to free - dom._____

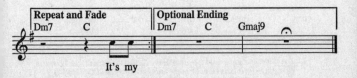

Repeat and Fade | **Optional Ending**
Dm7   C | Dm7   C   Gmaj9

It's my

BREATHE ON ME

Words and Music by GRANT CUNNINGHAM
and MATT HUESMANN

Breathe on me, breath of God;___ bring my life
Breathe on me, breath of God;___ I am a
Breathe on me, breath of God;___ cov - er my

close____ to____ Your Spir - it.
ves - sel____ to be filled._
sin____ with____ Your mer - cy.____

Beat in me, heart of God;___ my soul's in
Com - fort me, peace of God;___ Lord, I am
Speak to me, Word of God;___ give me a

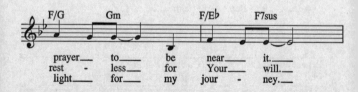

prayer____ to____ be near____ it.____
rest - less____ for Your____ will.____
light____ for____ my jour - ney.____

Fo - cus my___ eyes___ to___ on -
Si - lence my___ fears___ so that I___
Show me Your___ way___ and___ draw

To Coda ⊕

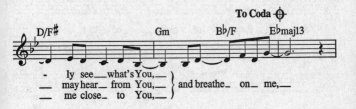

- ly see___ what's You,___
- may hear___ from You,___ } and breathe___ on___ me,___
- me close___ to You,___

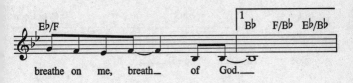

breathe on me, breath___ of God.___

Oh,___ oh, oh.___

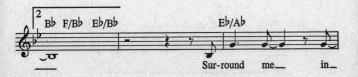

Sur - round me___ in___

30

Your glo - ry, make Your pres - ence known.

Set the path of grace be - fore me,

let Your breath be -

come my own.

D.C. al Coda

CODA

breathe on me,

breathe on me, breath of God.

Ah.

CAN'T LIVE A DAY

Words and Music by TY LACY,
CONNIE HARRINGTON and JOE BECK

I could live life a - lone___ and nev - er fill___ the long -
I could trav - el the world,___ see all the won - ders beau -

- ings of___ my heart,___ the
- ti - ful___ and new.___ They'd

heal - ing warmth___ of some - one's___ arms. And I___
on - ly make___ me think___ of___ You. And I___

could live with - out___ dreams,
could have all life___ of -

and nev - er know___ the thrill___
fered, rich - es that___ were far___

of what___ could be___ with
be - yond___ com - pare,___ to

ev - 'ry star__ so far__ and out__ of reach.__
grant my ev - 'ry wish__ with - out__ a care.__

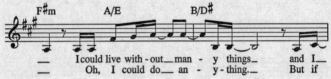

__ I could live with - out__ man - y things__ and I__
__ Oh, I could do__ an - y - thing.__ But if

__ could car - ry on.__ But }
You weren't in__ it all,__ } I could - n't face__

__ my life__ to - mor - row with - out Your hope__

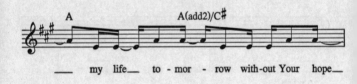

__ in my__ heart. I__ know__ I

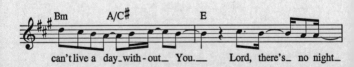

can't live a day__ with - out__ You.__ Lord, there's__ no night__

CAN'T KEEP A GOOD MAN DOWN

Words and Music by EDDIE CARSWELL,
LEONARD AHLSTROM and RUSS LEE

Moderately

He said good - bye to the an - gels of heav - en and He
I hear you say that it all sounds cra - zy; "It's a

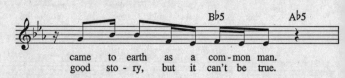

came to earth as a com - mon man.
good sto - ry, but it can't be true.

He taught us how we could love one an - oth - er, there was
How could a man who was dead and bur - ied mean a

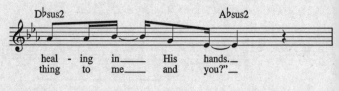

heal - ing in His hands.
thing to me and you?"

There were those who be - lieved and fol - lowed Him and
Here we are two thou-sand years la - ter and

37

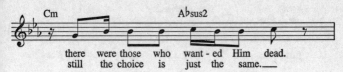

there were those who want-ed Him dead.
still the choice is just the same.___

They thought the grave would si - lence Him for-ev-er but
You can say that you don't_ be-lieve it, but it

they found out___ in - stead:___ }
does-n't change_ a_ thing.___ }
You can

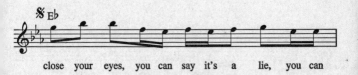

close your eyes, you can say it's a lie, you can

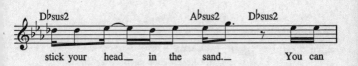

stick your head_ in the sand._ You can

turn a - way,_ e - ven try to ex - plain, "He was

38

just an - oth - er___ man."_ When they

nailed Him to the cross by His hands and His feet and they

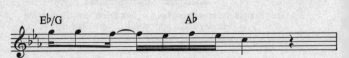

put Him in___ the ground,___

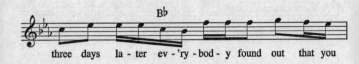

three days la - ter ev - 'ry - bod - y found out that you

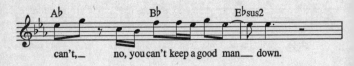

can't,___ no, you can't keep a good man___ down.

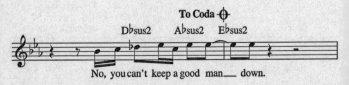

No, you can't keep a good man___ down.

I can

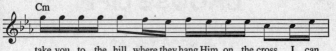

Cm

take you to the hill where they hang Him on the cross, I can

Ab

take you to the emp - ty tomb._____ I can

Cm

tell you He's a - live, 'cause He lives in me, but the

Dbsus2   Abus2   Eb

rest is up__ to you.__ (Na na, na na na,

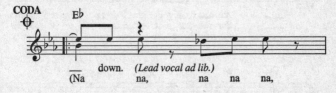

Dbsus2   Ab   Eb   **D.S. al Coda**

na na na na na na na na na. Na na, na na na.) You can

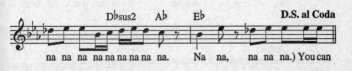

CODA

Eb

__ down. *(Lead vocal ad lib.)*
(Na na, na na na,

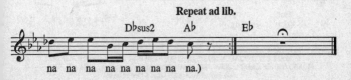

Repeat ad lib.

Dbsus2   Ab   Eb

na na na na na na na na na.)

CHOOSE LIFE

Words and Music by BILL BATSTONE
and STEVE WIGGINS

Moderately

A choice is set be-fore___ you now:___
Trust the Lord with all___ your heart,___

___ with liv-ing or dy - ing, bless-ing or
___ with all of your soul_____ and all of your

curs - ing. And now the time has come_ a-round
be - ing. Hold on, lis-ten and_ o-bey.

___ to turn from your fight - ing and rest in His
Sur - ren-der your life_____ in - to His

mer - cy. } Choose life___ that you might_ live.
keep - ing. }

The life that He_ gives,_ He gives you for-ev-

-er. Choose life,_ the way that is_ true,_

_ from the One who chose_ you,_

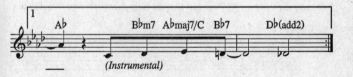

_ your Fa-ther in heav - en. Choose life._

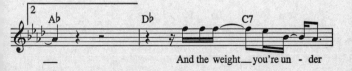

(Instrumental)

And the weight_you're un - der

42

GOD

Words and Music by REBECCA ST. JAMES
and TEDD TJORNHOM

Moderately fast

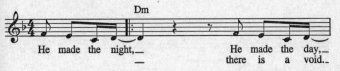

He made the night,__ He made the day,__ there is a void.__

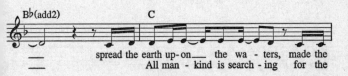

__ spread the earth up-on__ the wa - ters, made the
__ All man - kind is search - ing for the

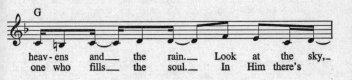

heav - ens and__ the rain.__ Look at the sky,__
one who fills__ the soul.__ In Him there's

__ see its de - sign;__ the
hope, in Him there's life. The

ver - y same__ Cre - a - tor is the
world cries for a Sav - ior that's

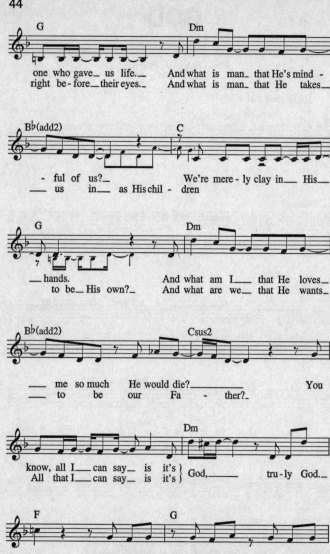

one who gave_ us life._ And what is man_ that He's mind -
right be - fore_ their eyes._ And what is man_ that He takes_

- ful of us?_ We're mere - ly clay in_ His_
_ us in_ as His chil - dren

_ hands. And what am I_ that He loves_
to be_ His own?_ And what are we_ that He wants_

_ me so much He would die?_____ You
_ to be our Fa - ther?_

know, all I_ can say_ is it's } God,_____ tru - ly God._
All that I_ can say_ is it's }

_ Can you see, can you hear, can you touch,

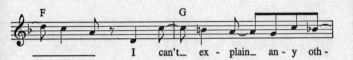

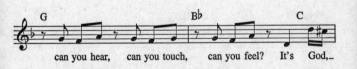

45

can you feel? It's God,___ tru - ly God.___

_____ I can't__ ex - plain__ an - y oth -

1. Bb C Dm
- er way_'cause it's God. *(Instrumental)*

2. Bb C
In-side us all,___ - er way_'cause it's

God,___ tru - ly God.___ Can you see,

can you hear, can you touch, can you feel? It's God,_

_ tru - ly God.___ I can't_

CIRCLE OF FRIENDS

Words and Music by DOUGLAS McKELVEY
and STEVE SILER

Warmly

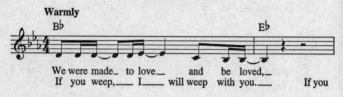

We were made to love_ and be loved,_ If you
If you weep,_ I_ will weep with you._

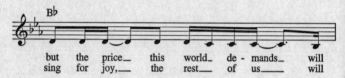

but the price_ this world_ de-mands_ will
sing for joy,_ the rest_ of us_ will

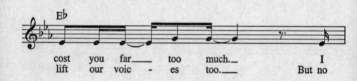

cost you far_ too much._ I
lift our voic-es too._ But no

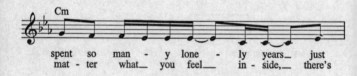

spent so man-y lone-ly years_ just
mat-ter what_ you feel_ in-side,_ there's

try-ing to_ fit_ in._ Now I've
no need to_ pre-tend._ That's the

50

A-mong the na - tions, tribes_ and tongues,_ we have sis - ters_ and broth - ers. And when we meet_ in heav - en, we will rec - og - nize_ each oth - er_____ with joy so_ deep_ and love so_ sweet._ Oh, we'll

51

cel - e - brate___ these friends___ and a

life that nev - er___ ends.___ In a cir - cle___ of

CODA

___ That it will not___ be long___ be-fore___

all will en - ter in___ to the shel - ter of___ this

cir - cle___ of friends.___

Cir - cle___ of friends.___

DEEPER

Words and Music by MARTIN SMITH
and STUART GARRARD

Moderate Rock Shuffle

I want to go deep-er, but I
deep-er, but is it

don't know how to swim.__ I want to be
just a stu-pid whim?__ I want to be

meek-er, but have you seen this old earth? I want to fly__
weak-er, be a help to the strong. I want to run__

__ high-er, but these arms
__ fast-er, but this old leg__

__ won't take__ me there.__ I want to be,
__ won't car-ry me.__ I want to be,

I want to be.__⎫
I want to be.__⎭

DIVE

Words and Music by
STEVEN CURTIS CHAPMAN

Moderately fast

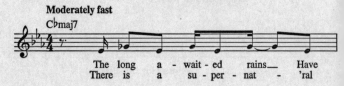

The long a - wait - ed rains___ Have
There is a su - per - nat - 'ral

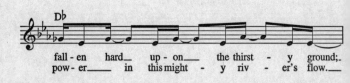

fall - en hard___ up - on___ the thirst - y ground;_
pow - er___ in this might - y riv - er's flow._

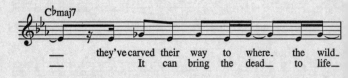

___ they've carved their way to where_ the wild_
___ It can bring the dead_ to life_

___ and rush - ing riv - er can_ be found._
___ and it_ can fill_ an emp - ty soul_

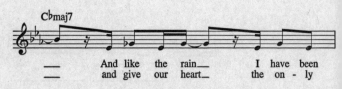

___ And like the rain_ I have been
___ and give our heart_ the on - ly

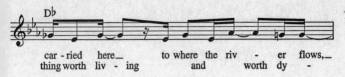

Db

car - ried here___ to where the riv - er flows,___
thing worth liv - ing and worth dy -

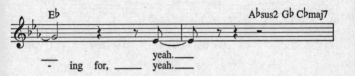

Eb   Absus2 Gb Cbmaj7

- ing for, ___ yeah.___
___ ing for, ___ yeah.___

My heart is rac - ing and my
But we will nev - er know___ the awe -

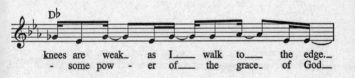

Db

knees are weak___ as I___ walk to___ the edge.___
- some pow - er of___ the grace___ of God___

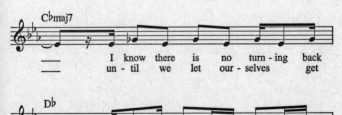

Cbmaj7

___ I know there is no turn - ing back
___ un - til we let our - selves get

Db

a - once my feet___ have left___ the ledge.___
swept a - way___ in - to___ this ho - ly flood.___

58

FOR THE GLORY
OF YOUR NAME

Words and Music by JOHN HARTLEY
and GARY SADLER

FRIENDS

Words and Music by MICHAEL W. SMITH
and DEBORAH D. SMITH

Moderately

Pack-ing up__ the dreams__ God plant-ed
With the faith__ and love____ God's giv-en

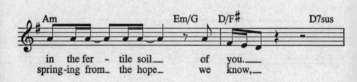

in the fer - tile soil__ of you.___
spring-ing from__ the hope__ we know,__

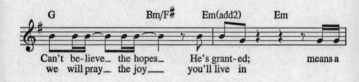

Can't be-lieve__ the hopes__ He's grant-ed; means a
we will pray__ the joy____ you'll live in

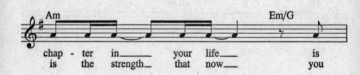

chap - ter in_____ your life__ is
is the strength__ that now__ you

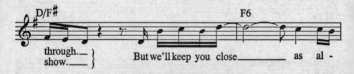

through.__ }
show.__ } But we'll keep you close_____ as al -

Bsus ... B

hard to let___ you go,___ in the

Esus ... Em ... C(add2)

Fa-ther's hands___ we know___ that a

Am7 ... D7sus

life-time's not___ too long___ to live___ as friends.___

[1] G ... D/F# ... C(add2)/E C/E D7sus [2] G ... Eb Db/Eb

___ ___ And___

Ab ... Eb/G

friends are friends___ for - ev - er if the

Db(add2)/F ... Db/F ... Eb7sus ... Eb7

Lord's___ the Lord___ of them.___ And a

Ab ... Eb/G

friend will not___ say "nev - er" 'cause the

Db(add2)/F   Db/F   Eb7sus   Eb7

wel - come will___ not end.___ Though it's

Csus   C

hard to let___ you go,___ in the

Fsus(add2)   Fm   Db(add2)   Db

Fa - ther's hands___ we know___ that a

Bbm7

life - time's not___ too long___

Eb7sus   C7/E   Fm(add2)   Fm

to live___ as friends.___ No, a

Bbm7   Eb7sus/Bb   Eb7sus

life-time's not___ too long___ to live___ as friends.___

Ab   Eb/G   Db/F   Ebsus Eb   Ab

___ (Instrumental)

GET DOWN

Words and Music by
AUDIO ADRENALINE

Moderately fast

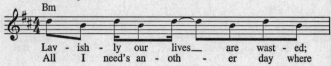

Lav - ish - ly our lives— are wast - ed;
All I need's an - oth - er day where

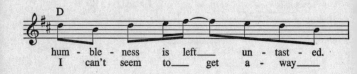

hum - ble - ness is left— un - tast - ed.
I can't seem to— get a - way—

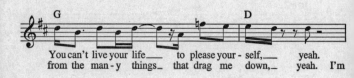

You can't live your life— to please your - self,— yeah.
from the man - y things— that drag me down,— yeah. I'm

That's a tip from my mis - take,— ex -
sure you've had a day like me— when

act - ly what it does - n't take. To
noth - in' seems to set you free from

67

68

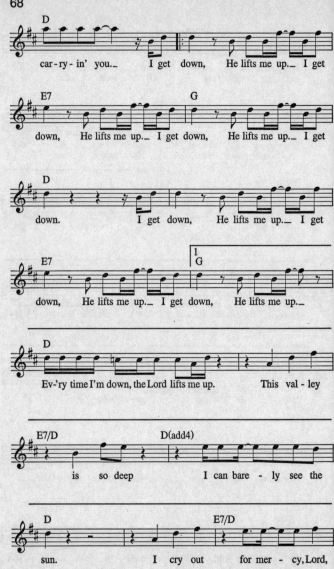

carry-in' you.__ I get down, He lifts me up.__ I get

down, He lifts me up.__ I get down, He lifts me up.__ I get

down. I get down, He lifts me up.__ I get

down, He lifts me up.__ I get down, He lifts me up.__

Ev'ry time I'm down, the Lord lifts me up. This val-ley

is so deep I can bare-ly see the

sun. I cry out for mer-cy, Lord,

GO AND SIN NO MORE

Words and Music by REBECCA ST. JAMES,
TEDD TJORNHOM and MICHAEL ANDERSON

Moderately

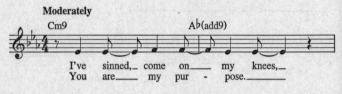

I've sinned,_ come on_ my knees,_
You are_ my pur - pose._

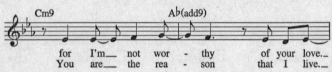

for I'm not wor - thy of your love._
You are_ the rea - son that I live._

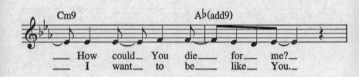

_ How could_ You die_ for_ me?_
_ I want_ to be_ like_ You._

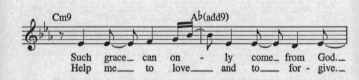

Such grace_ can on - ly come_ from God.
Help me_ to love_ and to_ for - give._

_ Oh Lord, You search_ me and know me.
_ God, let me not_ be dis - tract - ed.

You see me in - side out.___
Lord, help me fo - cus on You.

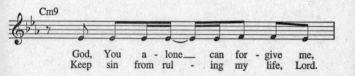

God, You a - lone___ can for - give me,
Keep sin from rul - ing my life, Lord.

e - rase my fear___ and my doubt.___ }
Make me___ ho - ly and pure.___ }

Fa - ther, You pick___ me up.___ I

feel like a child___ in Your arms.

I don't de - serve___ this love,___ but

I hear Your voice,__ Lord Je - sus.

"Go and sin no__ more." He said,

"I will not con - demn__ you. I'll for -

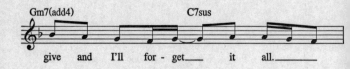

give and I'll for - get__ it all.__

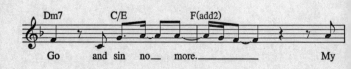

Go and sin no__ more.__ My

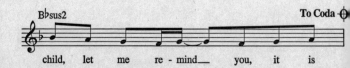

child, let me re - mind__ you, it is

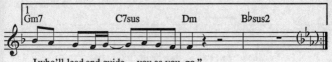

1

| Gm7 | C7sus | Dm | B♭sus2 |

I who'll lead and guide_ you as you go."

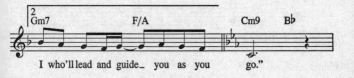

2

| Gm7 | F/A | Cm9 | B♭ |

I who'll lead and guide_ you as you go."

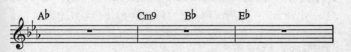

| A♭ | Cm9 | B♭ | E♭ |

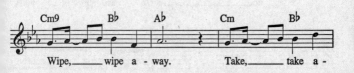

| Cm9 | B♭ | A♭ | Cm | B♭ |

Wipe,____ wipe a - way.   Take,____ take a -

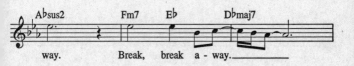

| A♭sus2 | Fm7 | E♭ | D♭maj7 |

way.   Break,   break a - way.____

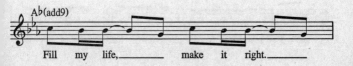

| A♭(add9) |

Fill   my   life,____   make   it   right.____

74

D.S. al Coda

N.C.

Fa-ther, help_ me, Fa - ther, help_ me go.

CODA

Gm7　　　　　C7sus　　　　F

I who'll lead and guide_ you as you go."

B♭sus2

He said,　　"I will not con - demn you,___

Gm7(add4)　C7sus　　　　　　F

no.___　　　　　　Go　　and sin no_ more.

B♭sus2

My child, let me re - mind_ you, it is

C7sus

I　who'll lead　and　guide_　you　as　you

F(add2)

go!" I've sinned, come on_ my knees._ How could_

GO LIGHT YOUR WORLD

Words and Music by
CHRIS RICE

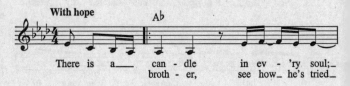

There is a___ can-dle in ev-'ry soul;___
broth-er, see how___ he's tried___

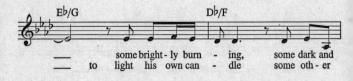

___ some bright-ly burn-ing, some dark and
___ to light his own can-dle some oth-er

cold.___ There is a___
way.___ See now your___

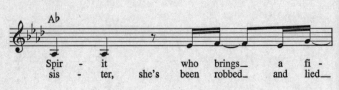

Spir - it who brings___ a fi-
sis - ter, she's been robbed___ and lied___

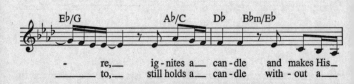

- re,___ ig - nites a___ can-dle and makes His___
___ to,___ still holds a___ can-dle with - out a___

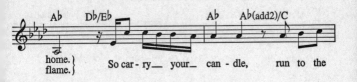

home.)
flame.)   So car - ry___ your___ can - dle,   run to the

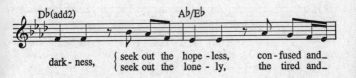

dark - ness, {seek out the hope - less,   con - fused and___
              {seek out the lone - ly,   the tired and___

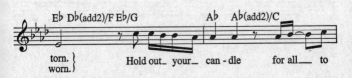

torn. } Hold out___ your___ can - dle   for all___ to
worn. }

see   it.   Take your can - dle   and go light your___

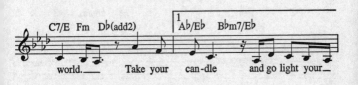

world.___   Take your   can - dle   and go light your___

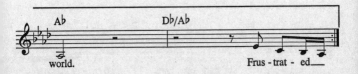

world.   Frus - trat - ed___

can - dle,   run to the dark - ness, { seek out the / seek out the

help-less, de -ceived and_ poor. } / hope-less, con -fused and_ torn. }   Hold out_ your_

can - dle   for all_ to see it.   Take your

1

can -dle   and go light your_ world.   Car-ry_ your_

2

can -dle   and go light your_ world._   Take your

can - dle_   and go light your_

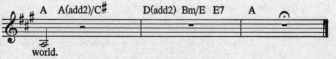

world.

GOD IS IN CONTROL

Words and Music by
TWILA PARIS

Steadily, with drive

This is__ no time for fear; this is__ a
His- to- ry march- es on, there is__ a

time for__ faith and de- ter- min- a- tion.
bot- tom__ line drawn a- cross the__ ag- es.

Don't lose__ the vi- sion here, car- ried__ a-
Cul- ture__ can make__ its plan, oh, but the__

way by__ the mo- tion. Hold on__ to
line nev- er chang- es. No mat- ter

all that__ you hide in__ your heart. There is__ one
how the__ de- cep- tion may fly, there is__ one

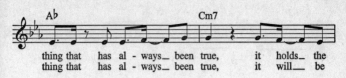

thing that has al - ways_ been true, it holds_ the
thing that has al - ways_ been true, it will_ be

world to-geth - er:_ }
true for-ev - er:_ }

God_ is in_ con-trol._

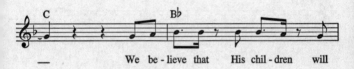

_ We be - lieve that His chil - dren will

not be_ for-sak - en. God_ is in_ con-trol._

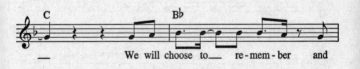

_ We will choose to_ re-mem - ber and

nev - er be shak - en. There is_ no pow - er_ a-

bove or____ be - side Him.____ We

know, oh,_____ God is in__ con - trol.__

__ Oh,_____ God is in__ con - trol.__

__ *(Instrumental)*

He has nev-er let you down; why start to wor-ry now? Why start to wor-ry now? He is still the Lord of all we see, and

He is still the lov-ing Fa-ther

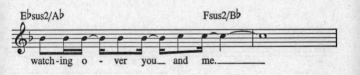

watch-ing o-ver you and me.

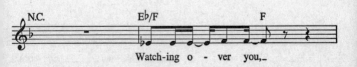

Watch-ing o-ver you,

84

THE GREAT ADVENTURE

**Words and Music by STEVEN CURTIS CHAPMAN
and GEOFF MOORE**

_ bolt. I saw a big fron - tier in front

of me, and I heard_ some -bod - y say,

"Let's_ go!"_____ Sad - dle up your

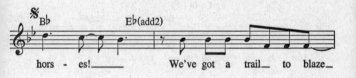

hors - es!_____ We've got a trail_ to blaze_

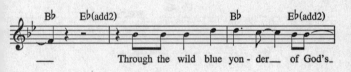

_ Through the wild blue yon - der_ of God's_

_ a - maz - ing_ grace._____

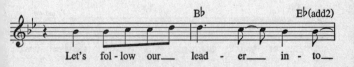

Let's fol - low our_ lead - er_ in - to_

90

THE GREAT DIVIDE

Words and Music by MATT HUESMANN
and GRANT CUNNINGHAM

With hope

Si - lence, tryin' to fath - om the
faith - ful, on my own I'm un -

dis - tance, look-ing out 'cross the can - yon carved by
a - ble. He found me hope-less, a - lone,__ and sent a

my__ hands. God is gra-cious; sin would still sep - a -
Sav - ior. He's pro - vid - ed a path and prom-ised to

rate us, were it not for the bridge His grace has
guide us safe - ly past all the sin that would di -

made_____ us.__ His love_____ will car - ry
vide_____ us.__ His love_____ de - liv - ers

me. }
me. } There's a bridge__ to cross__ the great__ di - vide,

GREAT EXPECTATIONS

Words and Music by
STEVEN CURTIS CHAPMAN

Moderately

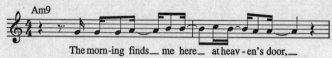

The morn-ing finds____ me here____ at heav-en's door,____

a place I've been so man-y times____ be-fore.

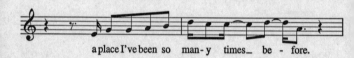

Fa-mil-iar thoughts____ and phras-es start to flow____

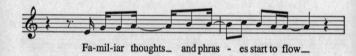

and car-ry me____ to plac-es that I know____   so____

____ well.____

But dare I go____ where I____
So wake the hope____ that slum-

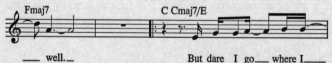

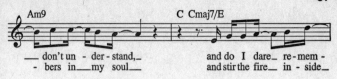

_ don't un - der - stand,_ and do I dare_ re-mem-
- bers in_ my soul_ and stir the fire_ in - side_

- ber where_ I am?_ I stand be-fore_ the great_
_ and make_ it grow._ I'm trust-ing in_ a love_

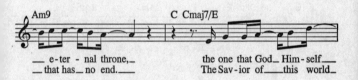

_ e-ter - nal throne,_ the one that God_ Him-self_
_ that has_ no end._ The Sav-ior of_ this world_

_ is seat - ed on,_ and I,_ I've been in-vit-
_ has called me friend,_ and I,_ I've been in-vit-

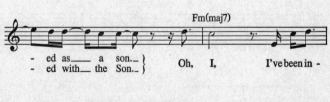

- ed as_ a son._ ⎫ Oh, I, I've been in -
- ed with_ the Son._ ⎭

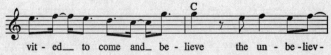

vit - ed_ to come and_ be - lieve the un - be -liev-

- a - ble, re - ceive the in - con - ceiv-

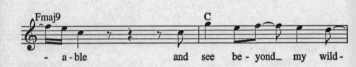

- a - ble and see be - yond__ my wild-

- est i - mag - i - na - tions. Lord,__ I

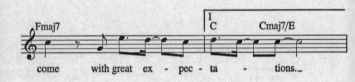

come with great ex - pec - ta - tions.__

(Great ex - pec - ta - tions.)__

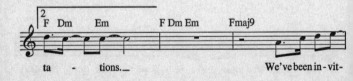

ta - tions.__ We've been in - vit-

- ed with the Son, and we've been in -

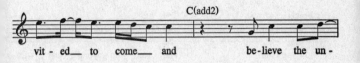

vit - ed to come and be - lieve the un -

- be - liev - a - ble, re - ceive the in -

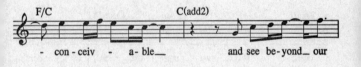

- con - ceiv - a - ble and see be - yond our

wild - est i - mag - i - na - tion. Lord, we

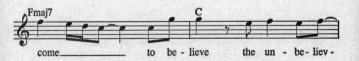

come to be - lieve the un - be - liev -

- a - ble,   re - ceive the in - con - ceiv-

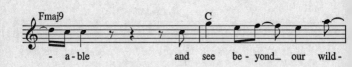

- a - ble   and see be - yond_ our wild-

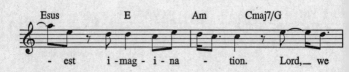

- est i - mag - i - na - tion. Lord,_ we

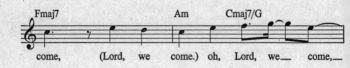

come,   (Lord, we   come.) oh, Lord, we_ come,_

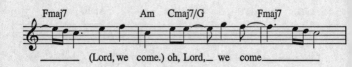

_____ (Lord, we come.) oh, Lord,_ we come_____

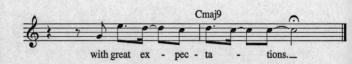

with great ex - pec - ta - tions._

HEAVEN IN THE REAL WORLD

Words and Music by
STEVEN CURTIS CHAPMAN

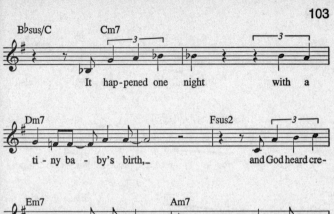

It hap-pened one night with a

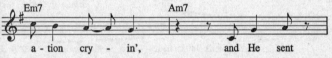

ti - ny ba - by's birth,_ and God heard cre-

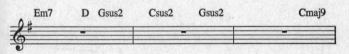

a - tion cry - in', and He sent

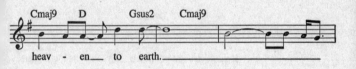

heav - en_ to earth._

He is the hope,_ He is the peace_

HERE I AM

Words and Music by REBECCA ST. JAMES, BILL DEATON and ERIC CHAMPION

Moderate Rock

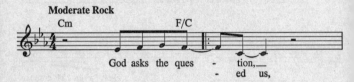

God asks the ques - tion,___
- ed us,

"Whom shall__ I send?"___
"Go and tell the Good News,___

Now, what will we an - swer?___ Will we
for the har- vest is man - y,___ but the

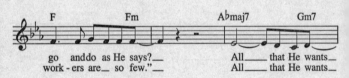

go and do as He says?___ All___ that He wants___
work-ers are__ so few."___ All___ that He wants

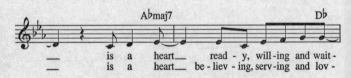

___ is a heart__ read - y, will-ing and wait-
___ is a heart__ be - liev - ing, serv-ing and lov -

- ing. }
- ing Him. }   Here I am,___ I sur-ren-

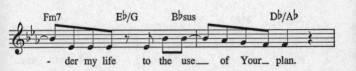

-der my life to the use___ of Your___ plan.

Here I am,___ I will do___

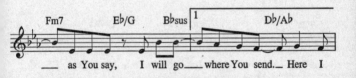

___ as You say, I will go___ where You send.___ Here I

am.___ Je-sus com-mand-___ where You___ send.

Here I___ am,___ I sur-ren-

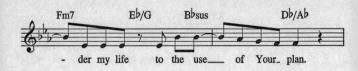

Fm7   Eb/G   Bbsus   Db/Ab

- der my life   to the use___ of Your_ plan.

Cm   Bb/D   Eb

Here   I   am,___   I   will   do___

To Coda ⊕

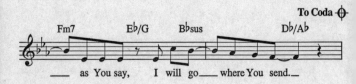

Fm7   Eb/G   Bbsus   Db/Ab

___ as You say,   I will go___ where You send.___

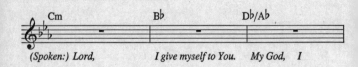

Cm   Bb   Db/Ab

(Spoken:) Lord,   *I give myself to You.*   *My God,*   *I*

Ab   Cm   Bb

trust You.   *Lord, tell me Your ways.*   *Show me how to live.*

D.S. al Coda   **CODA**
(take 2nd ending)   ⊕

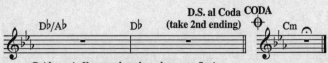

Db/Ab   Db   Cm

Guide me in Your truth and teach me, my Savior.

HIS STRENGTH IS PERFECT

Words and Music by STEVEN CURTIS CHAPMAN
and JERRY SALLEY

110

HOW BEAUTIFUL

Words and Music by
TWILA PARIS

Moderately, with feeling

How beau - ti - ful_____ the hands___ that___
beau - ti - ful_____ the heart___ that___
beau - ti - ful_____ the ra - diant___

served_____ the wine and the bread___ and the
bled,_____ that took all my___ sin and
Bride_____ who waits for her___ Groom with His

sons_ of the earth. How_____ beau - ti -
bore_ it in - stead. How_____ beau - ti -
light_ in her eyes. How_____ beau - ti -

ful the feet_____ that___ walked the
ful the ten - der___ eyes that
ful when hum - ble hearts___ give the

long dust - y___ roads and the hill___ to the
choose to for - give and nev - er___ de -
fruit of pure_ lives so that oth - ers___ may

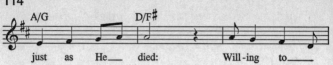

just as He___ died: Will-ing to___

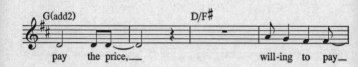

pay the price,___ will-ing to pay___

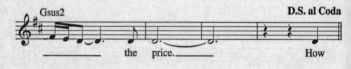

_____ the price.___ How

CODA

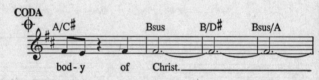

bod-y of Christ.___

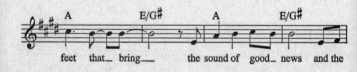

___ How beau - ti-ful___ the

feet that___ bring___ the sound of good___ news and the

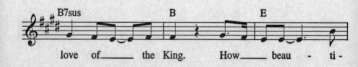

love of___ the King. How___ beau - ti-

I SURRENDER ALL

**Words and Music by DAVID MOFFITT
and REGIE HAMM**

With conviction

I have wres-tled in the dark - ness of this
source of my am - bi - tion is the

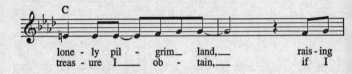

lone - ly pil - grim land, rais-ing
treas - ure I ob - tain, if I

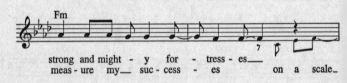

strong and might - y for - tress - es on a scale
meas - ure my suc - cess - es on a scale

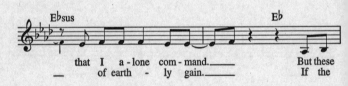

that I a - lone com - mand. But these
of earth - ly gain. If the

cas - tles I've con - struct - ed by the
fo - cus of my vi - sion is the

118

now be-longs_ to You;_ the life_ I

live is not_ my own._ Just as

A-bra-ham_ laid I-saac_ on the

sac-ri-fi-cial_ fire,_ if

all I have_ is all that You_ de-sire,_

_ I sur-ren - der all._

IF I STAND

Words and Music by RICH MULLINS
and STEVE CUDWORTH

Rhythmically

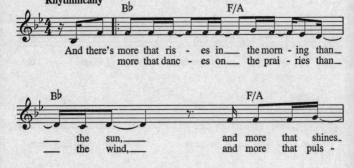

And there's more that ris - es in___ the morn - ing than___
more that danc - es on___ the prai - ries than___

___ the sun,___ and more that shines
___ the wind,___ and more that puls -

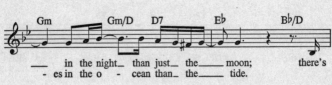

___ in the night___ than just___ the___ moon; there's
- es in the o - cean than___ the___ tide.

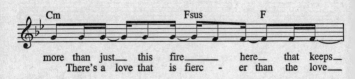

more than just___ this fire___ here___ that keeps
There's a love that is fierc - er than the love___

___ me___ warm in a shel -
___ be - tween___ friends; more___

123

125

IF THIS WORLD

Words and Music by MICHELLE TUMES,
TYLER HAYES, ERIC SUNDIN and MARK HEIMERMANN

Happily

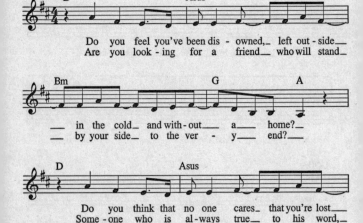

Do you feel you've been dis - owned,_ left out - side_
Are you look - ing for a friend_ who will stand_

_ in the cold_ and with - out_ a home?_
_ by your side_ to the ver - y end?_

Do you think that no one cares_ that you're lost_
Some - one who is al - ways true_ to his word,_

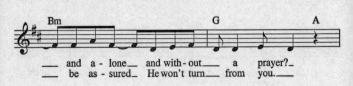

_ and a - lone_ and with - out_ a prayer?_
_ be as - sured_ He won't turn_ from you.

Don't give in_ to the lie_ that there's no
Put your faith_ in the One_ who will nev -

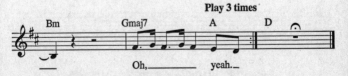

IF YOU WANT ME TO

Words and Music by GINNY OWENS
and KYLE MATTHEWS

Reflectively

Csus/G

The path - way___ is bro - ken and the

G   Am   Fsus2   Csus2/E

signs are un - clear. And___ I don't know the

G   Am

rea - son why You brought___ me here.___ But

F(add9)   Csus2/E

just be - cause___ You love___ me___ the

G   Am   Csus2/E   D7

way that You___ do, I'm___ gon-na walk___ through the

G   F/G   C

val - ley___ if You___ want___ me to.___

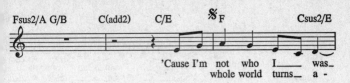

Fsus2/A G/B   C(add2)   C/E   %F   Csus2/E

'Cause I'm not who I___ was___
whole world turns___ a-

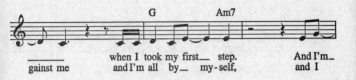

G   Am7

when I took my first___ step.   And I'm
gainst me   and I'm all by___ my-self,   and I

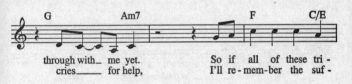

F   Csus2/E

___ cling - in' to the prom - ise You're___ not
can't___ hear___ You an - swer   my

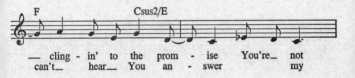

G   Am7   F   C/E

through with___ me yet.   So if   all of these tri -
cries___ for help,   I'll re - mem-ber the suf -

G   Am7

als___   bring me___ clos - er___ to You,___
fring___   that Your___ love___ put___ You through.__

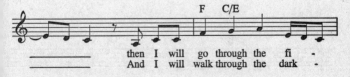

F   C/E

___   then I will go through the fi -
___   And I will walk through the dark -

132

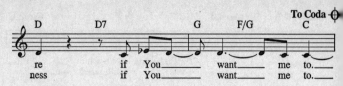

re — — if You____ want____ me to.____
ness — — if You____ want____ me to.____

— _(Instrumental)_

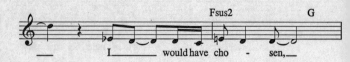

It may not be____ the way____

____ I____ would have cho - sen,____

when You lead me through____ a world____

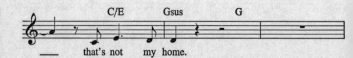

____ that's not my home.

But You nev-er said___ it would_ be eas - y,

You on - ly said___ I'll nev-er

go a-lone.   So when the

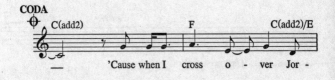

CODA

___   'Cause when I cross o - ver Jor -

- dan   I'm gon-na sing,   gon-na shout.

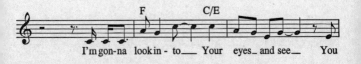

I'm gon-na lookin - to___ Your eyes_ and see___ You

nev-er let__ me down.__ So take me on the path-

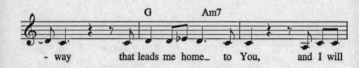

- way that leads me home__ to You, and I will

walk through the val - ley____ if You want____ me

to.____ *(Instrumental)*

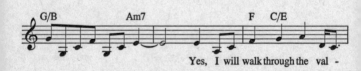

Yes, I will walk through the val -

ley__ if You__ want____ me to.

LIVE OUT LOUD

Words and Music by STEVEN CURTIS CHAPMAN and GEOFF MOORE

Moderate Rock

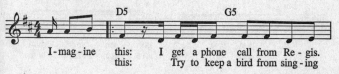

I - mag - ine this: I get a phone call from Re - gis.
this: Try to keep a bird from sing - ing

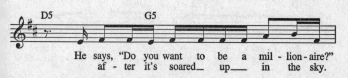

He says, "Do you want to be a mil - lion - aire?"
af - ter it's soared_ up_ in the sky.

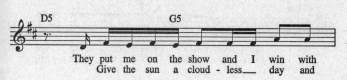

They put me on the show and I win with
Give the sun a cloud - less_ day and

two life - lines to spare. Now pic - ture
tell it not to shine. Now think a - bout

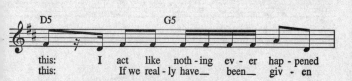

this: I act like noth - ing ev - er hap - pened
this: If we real - ly have_ been_ giv - en

D5   **G5**

and bur - y all the mon - ey in a cof - fee can.
the gift__ of a life__ that will nev - er end,

Bm   **A/C♯**

Well, I've been giv - en more than
and if we have been filled with

D   **D/F♯**   **G6/9**

Re - gis ev - er gave a - way.
liv - ing hope, we're gon - na o - ver - flow,

Bm   **A/C♯**

I was a dead man who was
and if God's love is burn - ing

D   **D/F♯**   **G6/9**

called to come out of my__ grave.
in our hearts we're gon - na__ glow.

Bm   **A/C♯**   **Gsus2**

And I think it's time for mak - in' some noise.__ }
There's just no way to keep it__ in.__ } Wake the

D   **G**   **D**   **G**

neigh - bors;__ get__ the word out.__ Come on,

C5 C#5 D5   Bm   Bbm Am G   Am Bbm

— (La,   la   la,

Bm   Bbm Am G   Am Bbm Bm   Bbm Am G

la   la   la la,   la   la   la,

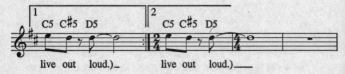

1. C5 C#5 D5   2. C5 C#5 D5

live out   loud.)   live out   loud.)

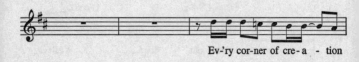

Ev-'ry cor-ner of cre-a - tion

is a liv - ing de-cla-ra - tion.

A5   B5   C5

Come   join   the   song   we   were   made

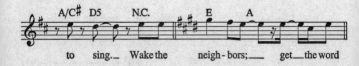

A/C# D5   N.C.   E   A

to   sing. Wake the   neigh-bors; get the word

JESUS WILL STILL
BE THERE

**Words and Music by ROBERT STERLING
and JOHN MANDEVILLE**

Things change,___ plans fail,___
Time flies,___ hearts turn,___ a

you look for love_ on a grand - er scale.___
lit - tle bit wis - er from les - sons learned.___

Storms rise,___ hopes fade,___ and
But some - times weak - ness wins, and

you place your bets___ on___ an - oth -
you lose your foot - hold___ once___

- er day.___ }
___ a - gain. }

When the

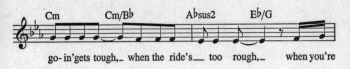

go-in'gets tough,_ when the ride's_ too rough,_ when you're

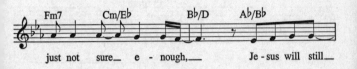

just not sure_ e - nough,_ Je - sus will still_

_ be_ there._ His love will nev - er change,_

_ sure as a stead - y rain._ Je - sus will still_

_ be_ there._ When no one else_ is true,_

_ He'll still be lov - ing you._ When it

looks like you've lost____ it____ all____

____ and you have-n't got____ a prayer,____

____ Je-sus will still____ be____ there.

____

____ be____ there.____

____ be____ there.____

____ Je-sus will still____ be____ there.____

____ His love will nev-er change, sure as a stead-

A LITTLE MORE

Words and Music by
JENNIFER KNAPP

Moderately

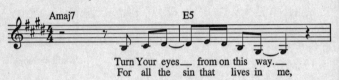

Turn Your eyes___ from on this way.___
For all the sin that lives in me,

I have proved___ to live a das-tard-ly day. I___
it took a nail to set___ me free. Still___

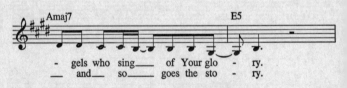

___ hid my face___ from the saints___ and the an-
___ what I do___ I___ don't___ wan-na do___

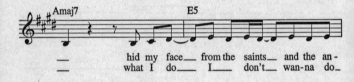

- gels who sing___ of Your glo___ - ry.
___ and___ so___ goes the sto - ry.

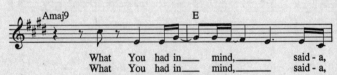

What You had in___ mind,___ said - a,
What You had in___ mind,___ said - a,

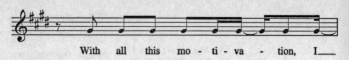

With all this mo-ti-va-tion, I

Am6/C

still find a hes-i-ta-tion

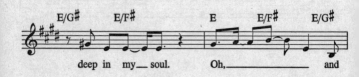

E/G#   E/F#   E   E/F#   E/G#

deep in my soul. Oh, and

Amaj7

de-spite all my de-mand-ing, I

Am6/C

still find You un-der-stand-ing.

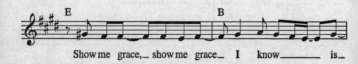

E   B

Show me grace, show me grace I know is

_____ a,

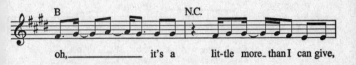

oh,_____ it's a   lit-tle more_ than I can give,

lit-tle more_ than I___ de-serve,__ un - earth_ this ho-

li-ness I   can't earn. It's a___   lit-tle more_ than I can give,

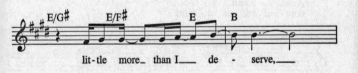

lit-tle   more_ than I___ de - serve,___

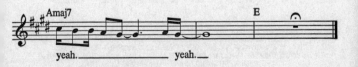

yeah._____ yeah._

MERCY CAME RUNNING

Words and Music by DAN DEAN,
DAVE CLARK and DON KOCH

Once there was a ho - ly___ place,___
Once there was a bro - ken___ heart,___

ev - i - dence___ of God's em - brace,___
way too hu - man from the___ start,___

and I can al - most see mer - - cy's___ face___
and all the years left it torn___ a - part,___

pressed a - gainst___ the veil.___
hope - less and___ a - fraid.___

Look - ing down with long - ing___ eyes,___
Walls I nev - er meant to___ build

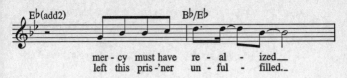

mer - cy must have re - al - ized___
left this pris -'ner un - ful - filled.___

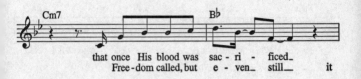

that once His blood was sac - ri - ficed___
Free - dom called, but e - ven___ still___ it

free - dom would___ pre - vail.___ And as the
seemed so far___ a - way.___ I was

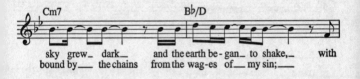

sky grew___ dark___ and the earth be - gan___ to shake,___ with
bound by___ the chains from the wag - es of___ my sin;___

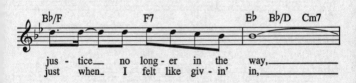

jus - tice___ no long - er in the way,___
just when___ I felt like giv - in' in,___

mer - cy came___ a - run - nin'___ like a pris -'ner set free,___

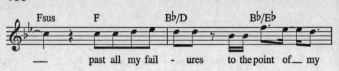

past all my fail - ures   to the point of __ my

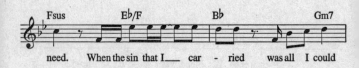

need.   When the sin that I __ car - ried   was all I could

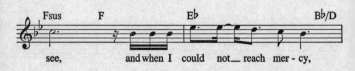

see,   and when I could not __ reach mer - cy,

mer - cy came __ a - run - nin' __ to me. __

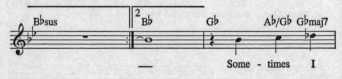

__   Some - times   I

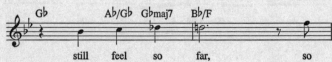

still   feel   so   far,   so

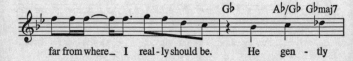

far from where __ I real - ly should be.   He gen - tly

calls to my heart_____ just to re-mind_

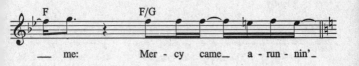

____ me: Mer - cy came___ a - run - nin'_

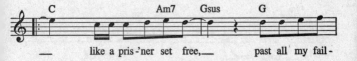

___ like a pris-'ner set free,___ past all my fail-

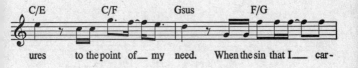

ures to the point of ___ my need. When the sin that I ___ car-

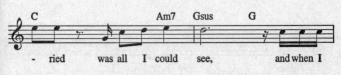

- ried was all I could see, and when I

could not_ reach mer - cy, mer - cy came,_ mer - cy came_ a - run - nin'_

mer - cy came_ a - run - nin'_ to me.___

THE MESSAGE

Words and Music by MICHAEL OMARTIAN,
MARK HARRIS and DON KOCH

The fields are white___ and now the time___
I can't ig - nore___ what's right be - fore___

___ has___ come,___ for there's___ a har -
___ my___ eyes,___ for all_____ a - round

- vest, there is work___ left to_____ be___
___ this work is search - in' for_____ a

done. Lord, here___ am I,_____
sign; Out - side___ the door_____ they're

I will be___ the one,___ I'm com -
liv - in' in___ the night,___ and the

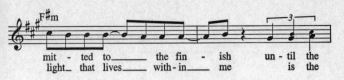

mit - ted to___ the fin - ish   un - til the
light_ that lives__ with-in__ me   is the

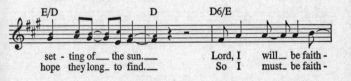

set-ting of_ the sun.__   Lord, I will_ be faith-
hope they long_ to find.__   So I must_ be faith-

- ful   in all_ I say_ and do.__
- ful   in all_ I say_ and do.__

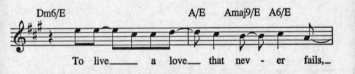

To live___ a love__ that nev - er fails,_

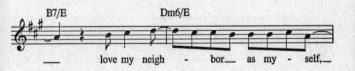

__ love my neigh - bor_ as my - self,_

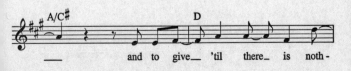

__ and to give_ 'til there_ is noth-

- in' left to give.

To live a faith that nev - er dies,

to be cru - ci - fied with

Christ; Un - til all

that lives through me is the mes - sage.

- sage.

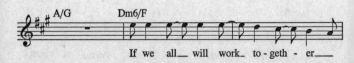

If we all will work to - geth - er

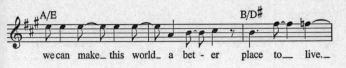

we can make this world a bet- er place to live.

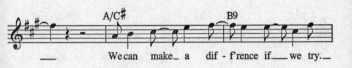

We can make a dif - f'rence if we try.

To live a love that nev - er fails,

love my neigh - bor as my - self,

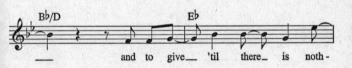

and to give 'til there is noth-

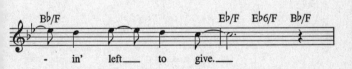

- in' left to give.

To live a faith that nev - er dies,

MY FAITH WILL STAY

Words and Music by
CHERI KEAGGY

Moderately

My faith will stay,___ my faith will grow,___

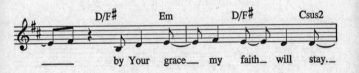

___ some-times fast some - times slow.

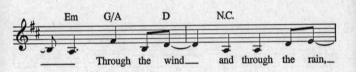

___ Through the wind___ and through the rain,

___ by Your grace___ my faith___ will stay.___

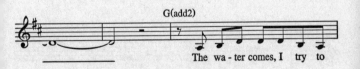

_____ The wa - ter comes, I try to

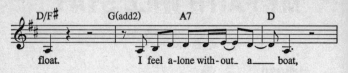

float.   I feel a-lone with-out_ a___ boat,

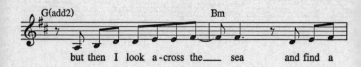

but then I look a-cross the___ sea   and find a

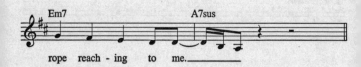

rope reach - ing to me._____

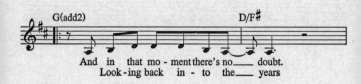

And in that mo - ment there's no___ doubt.
Look-ing back in - to the___ years

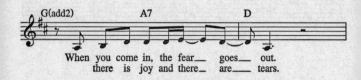

When you come in, the fear___ goes___ out.
there is joy and there___ are___ tears.

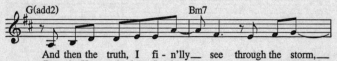

And then the truth, I fi - n'lly___ see through the storm,___
But in Your wis-dom I have___ grown, great - er strength_

MORE TO THIS LIFE

**Words and Music by STEVEN CURTIS CHAPMAN
and PHIL NAISH**

Moderate Rock

To - day I watched in si - lence as
night he lies in si - lence,

peo - ple passed me by, and I
star - ing in - to space, and

strained to see if there was some - thing
looks for ways to make to - mor - row

hid - den in their eyes. But they
bet - ter than to - day. But

all looked back at me as if to say:
in the morn - ing light it looks the same.

"Life just goes on."
"Life just goes on."

164

life than liv - in'___ and dy - in', more than___ just try-

- in' to make___ it through the day. More_____ to this___

life, more than___ these eyes_ a - lone___ can see,_ and there's more_

_ than this life_ a - lone_ can be._____

To-___

So where do___ we start___ to

find ev - 'ry part_ of what makes_ this_ life com -

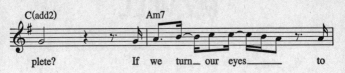

C(add2)   Am7

plete?   If we turn_ our eyes_____ to

Bm7   G(add2)/B   F6/9

Je - sus,___ we'll find___ life's true_ be - gin - ning is

C(add2)/E   Dsus   Dsus2

there_ at_ the_ cross where He___ died.___

D.S. al Coda

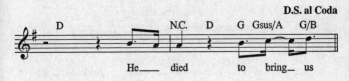

D   N.C.   D   G   Gsus/A   G/B

He___ died to bring_ us

CODA

Gsus2   C6/9

Gsus2

More to_ this life.___   More to this

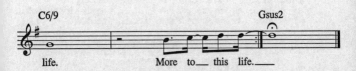

C6/9   Gsus2

life.   More to_ this life.___

MY WILL

Words and Music by TOBY McKEEHAN,
MICHAEL TAIT, JOEY ELWOOD and DANIEL PITTS

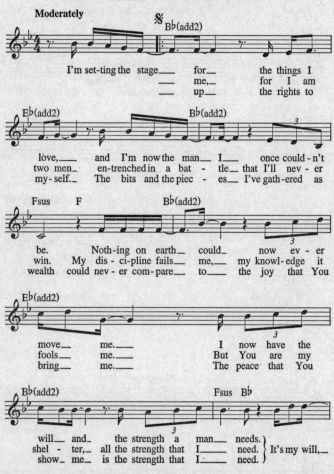

I'm set-ting the stage____ for____ the things I
____ me,____ for I am
____ up____ the rights to

love,____ and I'm now the man____ I____ once could-n't
two men____ en-trenched in a bat - tle that I'll nev - er
my-self.____ The bits and the piec - es____ I've gath-ered as

be.____ Noth-ing on earth____ could____ now ev - er
win.____ My dis - ci-pline fails____ me,____ my knowl-edge it
wealth could nev - er com-pare____ to____ the joy that You

move____ me.____ I now have the
fools____ me.____ But You are my
bring____ me.____ The peace that You

will____ and____ the strength a man____ needs.
shel - ter,____ all the strength that I____ need.
show____ me____ is the strength that I____ need.
It's my will,____

SHINE ON US

Words and Music by MICHAEL W. SMITH
and DEBBIE SMITH

170

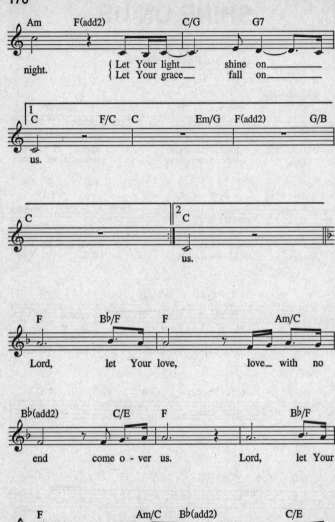

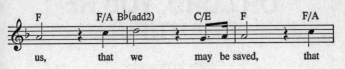

us,   that we   may be saved,   that

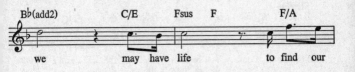

we   may have life   to find our

way_____ in the dark - est night.   Let Your love_

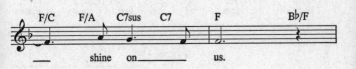

_   come o - ver us.   Let Your light_

_   shine on_____ us.

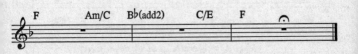

OH LORD, YOU'RE BEAUTIFUL

Words and Music by
KEITH GREEN

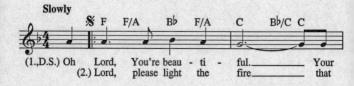

(1.,D.S.) Oh Lord, You're beau - ti - ful._____ Your
(2.) Lord, please light the fire_____ that

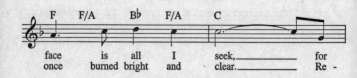

face is all I seek,_____ for
once burned bright and clear._____ Re -

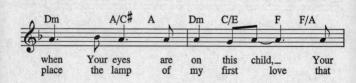

when Your eyes are on this child,__ Your
place the lamp of my first love that

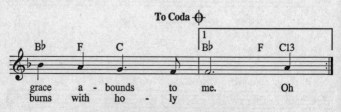

grace a - bounds to me. Oh
burns with ho - ly

PLACE IN THIS WORLD

Words by WAYNE KIRKPATRICK and AMY GRANT
Music by MICHAEL W. SMITH

Moderate Rock Ballad

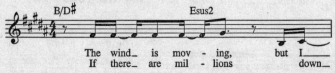

The wind_ is mov - ing, but I_____
If there_ are mil - lions down_____

_ am stand - ing still._ A life_ of pag - es
_____ on_ their knees,_ a - mong_ the man - y

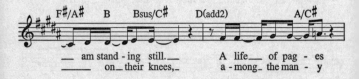

wait - ing to_____ be_ filled.
can You still_____ hear_ me?

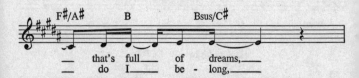

A heart_ that's hope - ful, a head_____
Hear_ me ask - ing where_____

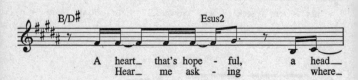

_ that's full_____ of dreams,_____
_ do I_____ be - long,_____

175

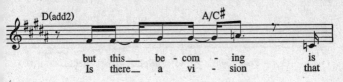

but this_ be - com - ing is
Is there_ a vi - sion that

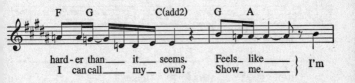

hard - er than_ it_ seems. Feels_ like_ } I'm
I can call_ my_ own? Show_ me._ }

look - ing for a rea - son, roam -

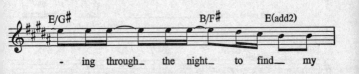

- ing through_ the night_ to find_ my

place in this world,_ my_ place_ in this world._

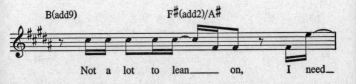

Not a lot to lean_ on, I need_

PRAY

Words and Music by REBECCA ST. JAMES,
MICHAEL QUINLAN and TEDD TJORNHOM

*Vocal written one octave higher than sung.

179

180

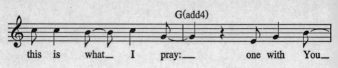

this is what_ I pray:_ one with You_

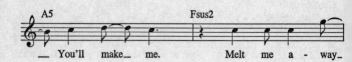

_ You'll make_ me. Melt me a - way_

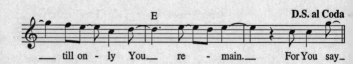

_ till on - ly You_ re - main._ For You say_

D.S. al Coda

CODA

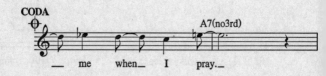

_ me when_ I pray._

Je - sus, I am bro - ken now_

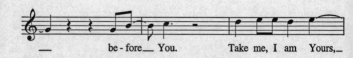

_ be - fore_ You. Take me, I am Yours,_

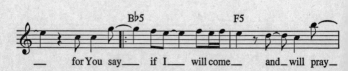

_ for You say_ if I_ will come_ and_ will pray_

RUN TO YOU

Words and Music by
TWILA PARIS

Moderately

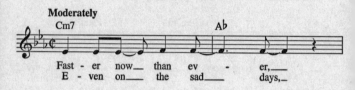

Fast - er now__ than ev - er,__
E - ven on__ the sad__ days,__

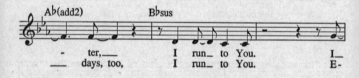

I run__ to You.
I run__ to You.

Now I know__ You bet -
E - ven on__ the good__

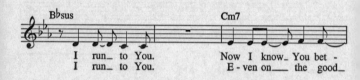

__ ter,__ I run__ to You. I__
__ days, too, I run__ to You. E -

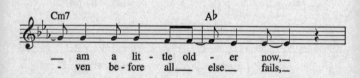

__ am a lit - tle old - er now,__
__ ven be - fore all__ else__ fails,__

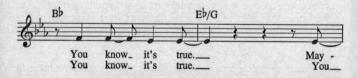

You know__ it's true.__
You know__ it's true.__

May - You -

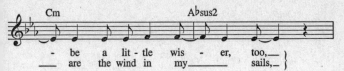

- be a lit - tle wis - er, too,___
___ are the wind in my___ sails,___ }

I run___ to You.___ And I___ can see___

___ (I___ can see)___ deep -

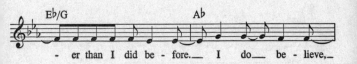

- er than I did be - fore.___ I do___ be - lieve,___

___ (I___ be - lieve)___ nev -

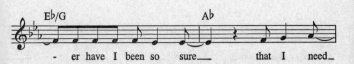

- er have I been so sure___ that I need___

You ev - 'ry { min - ute, ev - 'ry day,_
{ foot - step, all_ the way,_

That I need_ You more_ than I_
That I need_ You so_ much more_

could ev - er say._
than I can say._

Ooh,_____ I run_ to You._

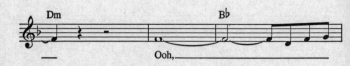

_ Ooh,_____

what else would_ I do?_ I run_ to You._

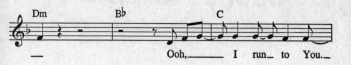

Ooh,____ I run__ to You.__

Ooh._____

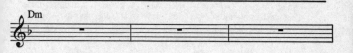

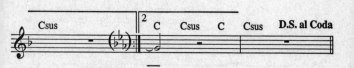

SECRET AMBITION

**Words and Music by MICHAEL W. SMITH,
WAYNE KIRKPATRICK and AMY GRANT**

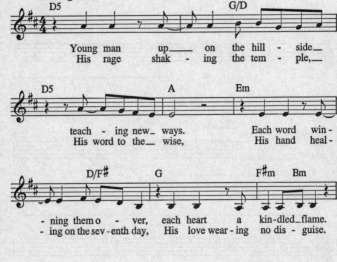

Driving Rock

Young man up___ on the hill - side___
His rage shak - ing the tem - ple,

teach - ing new_ ways.
His word to the_ wise,

Each word win -
His hand heal -

- ning them o - ver, each heart a kin-dled_flame.
- ing on the sev - enth day, His love wear - ing no dis - guise.

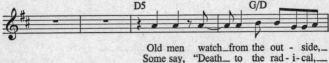

Old men watch_from the out - side,___
Some say, "Death_ to the rad - i - cal,___

guard - ing their_ prey.
He's way out of_ line!"

Threat-ened by the
Some say, "Praise_

voice of the par - a - gon / lead - ing___ their___
___ be the mir - a - cle! / God sends a

lambs a - way, / lead - ing___ them___
bless - ed___ sign, / a bless - ed sign___ for

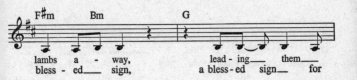

far a - way.___ /
trou - bled___ times."___ }

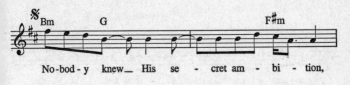

No - bod - y knew___ His se - cret am - bi - tion,

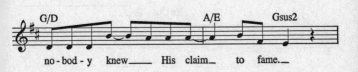

no - bod - y knew___ His claim___ to fame.___

He broke the old___ rules steeped___ in tra - di - tion,

188

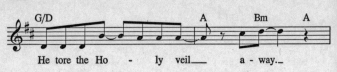

He tore the Ho - ly veil__ a - way._

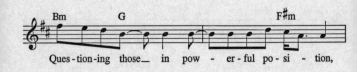

Ques - tion - ing those_ in pow - er - ful po - si - tion,

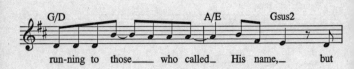

run - ning to those__ who called_ His name,_ but

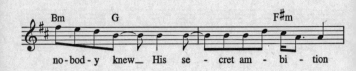

no - bod - y knew_ His se - cret am - bi - tion

was to give__ His life__ a - way._

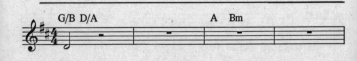

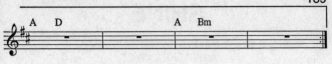

— a - way._____

Oh._____ Oh,_____ whoa.

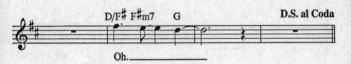

Oh._____

D.S. al Coda

CODA

— a - way._____

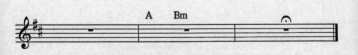

SHINE

**Words and Music by PETER FURLER
and STEVE TAYLOR**

Moderately

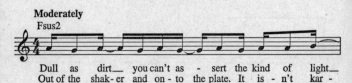

Dull as dirt___ you can't as - sert the kind of light___
Out of the shak- er and on-to the plate. It is - n't kar-

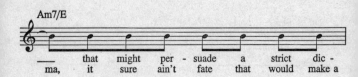

___ ma, that might per - suade a strict dic-
___ ma, it sure ain't fate that would make a

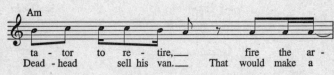

ta - tor to re - tire,___ fire the ar-
Dead - head sell his van.___ That would make a

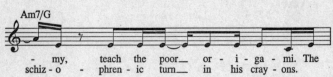

- my, teach the poor___ or - i - ga - mi. The
schiz - o - phren - ic turn___ in his cray - ons.

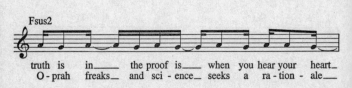

truth is in___ the proof is___ when you hear your heart___
O - prah freaks___ and sci - ence seeks a ra - tion - ale___

G5   C5

__ start ask - ing, "What's my mo - ti - va -tion?"
__ that shall ex - cuse this strange be - hav - ior.

Fsus2

And try as you may__ there is-n't a way to ex - plain__
When you let it shine__ you will in - spire the kind of

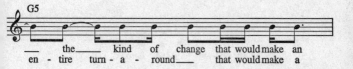

G5

__ the__ kind of change that would make an
en - tire turn - a - round__ that would make a

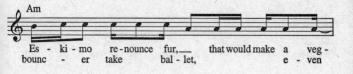

Am

Es - ki - mo re -nounce fur,__ that would make a veg -
bounc - er take bal - let, e - ven

- i - tar - i - an bar - be - cue ham - ster,
bounc - ers who aren't... hap - py. But

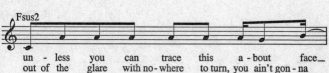

Fsus2

un - less you can trace this a - bout face__
out of the glare with no - where to turn, you ain't gon - na

G5

__ to a cer - tain sign. }
learn it on "What's My Line?" }

SING YOUR PRAISE
TO THE LORD

Words and Music by
RICHARD MULLINS

Sing your praise to__ the Lord,__ come on ev'ry-bod-y,

stand up and sing one more hal-le-lu-jah. Give your

praise to__ the Lord.__ I can nev-er tell you

just how much good that it's gon-na do__ ya just to

sing a-new the
sing a-loud the

song your heart__ learned to sing when He__ first gave His
song that some-one is dy-ing to hear__ down in the

195

and ev - er - more.

Praise Him, all___ you ser - vants. Give your

praise to___ the Lord,___ come on ev - 'ry - bod - y,

stand up and sing one more hal - le - lu - jah. Give your

praise to___ the Lord.___ I can nev - er tell you

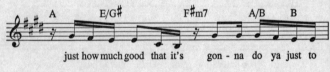

just how much good that it's gon - na do ya just to

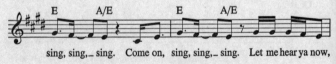

sing, sing,_ sing. Come on, sing, sing,_ sing. Let me hear ya now,

sing, sing,_ sing._____

SOMETIMES HE CALMS THE STORM

Words and Music by KEVIN STOKES
and TONY WOOD

Some - times He holds___ us close___ and lets the wind and waves__ go wild.___

Some - times He calms__ the storm___ and oth - er times__ He calms__ His child.

1 child,___ oh.___

2 child,___ oh.___

Some - times He calms__ the__ storm___

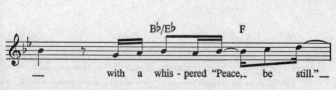

with a whis - pered "Peace,__ be still."___

And He can set - tle an - y

sea but it does - n't mean___ He will.

Some - times He holds___ us close___

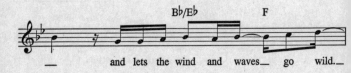

___ and lets the wind and waves___ go wild.___

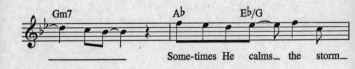

___ Some-times He calms___ the storm___

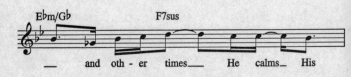

___ and oth - er times___ He calms___ His

child___

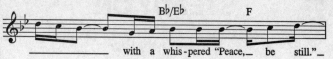

with a whis-pered "Peace,_ be still."_

_ And He can set - tle an - y sea,

but it does-n't mean_ He will.

Some - times He holds_ us close_

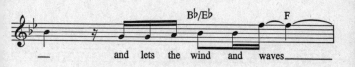

_ and lets the wind and waves_

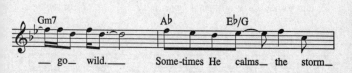

_ go_ wild._ Some-times He calms_ the storm_

_ and oth- er times_ He calms_ His child.

STEADY ON

Words and Music by GRANT CUNNINGHAM
and MATT HUESMANN

Moderately

Kick-ing up dust, heav-en or bust; we're
want to walk a while. We know that ev-'ry mile is

head-ed for the prom-ised land.__ Since the mo-
bring-ing us clos-er home.__ We want__

-ment we be-lieved, we've been ea-ger to leave,__ like a
__ to tell the sto-ry of sin-ners bound for glo-ry, and

child tug-ging dad-dy's hand.__ May we
turn to find we're not a-lone.__ When we

nev-er for-get that pa-tience__ is a vir-
walk in Your light, the lost will see You

- tue.____ Calm our anx-ious feet so
bet - ter.____ As the nar-row road gets

faith - ful hands__ can serve You, Lord.__
crowd - ed, won't You lead us stead-y on?__

__ } We run on up__ a - head,__

__ we lag be - hind You._____

__ It's hard to wait__ when heav-

- en's on our minds._____

Teach our rest - less feet__ to walk__ be -

side You,____ 'cause in our hearts we're

al - read-y gone.____

Will You walk with__ us, stead-y on?__

We

Stead-y me when the road__

of faith__ gets rock-y.__ Oh,__

read-y me for fears__ I can-not

THIS IS YOUR TIME

Words and Music by MICHAEL W. SMITH
and WES KING

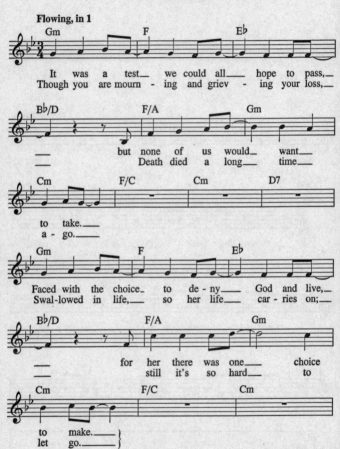

Flowing, in 1

It was a test__ we could all__ hope to pass,
Though you are mourn - ing and griev - ing your loss,

__ but none of us would__ want__
__ Death died a long__ time

to take.__
a - go.__

Faced with the choice__ to de - ny__ God and live,__
Swal-lowed in life,__ so her life__ car - ries on;

__ for her there was one__ choice
__ still it's so hard__ to

to make.__ }
let go.__ }

208

THIS MYSTERY

Words and Music by
NICHOLE NORDEMAN

Moderately

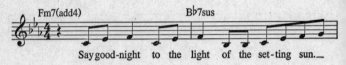

Say good-night to the light of the set-ting sun.__

One more day, one more__ way of keep-ing track__ of all I've

__ done.

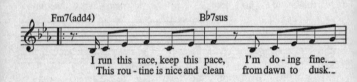

I run this race, keep this pace, I'm do-ing fine.
This rou-tine is nice and clean from dawn to dusk.__

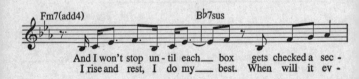

And I won't stop un-til each__ box gets checked a sec-
I rise and rest, I do my__ best. When will it ev-

ond time.___
er be e - nough?___

And life be-comes
And life be-comes

the 'round and 'round
the big - ger noise

re - volv - ing door___ that won't___
drown-ing out___ Your lit -

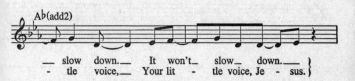

___ slow down.___ It won't___ slow___ down.___ }
- tle voice, Your lit - tle voice, Je - sus. }

Do You wish, do You want us to breathe a - gain?___

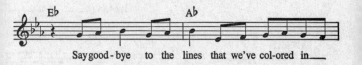

Say good - bye to the lines that we've col-ored in___

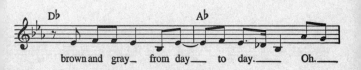

brown and gray___ from day___ to day.___ Oh.___

UNDO ME

Words and Music by
JENNIFER KNAPP

You don't have to say___ a thing.___ I can tell___ ___ by your eyes___ ex-act-ly what you mean. That it's

time___ to get down___ on my knees___ and pray,___ ___ "Lord, un - do___ me." Put a-way___ my flesh___

___ and___ bone.___ 'til You___ own___ this spir-it___ through___ me.

Lord, un - do_____ me.___

Ma - ma,— I know I made you cry,— but I never meant to hurt you, I nev - er meant to— lie.— While the world— shook its head— in shame,— I let you take the blame.— Broth-er,— I know you la-bored so— hard to— please,— yeah,— — yeah, yeah,— but I— cut you down— and I left— — you on your knees.— Well, I— know it must be

D.S. al Coda

218

Lord, I _____ am want - ing,__ need - ing,__ guilt - y__ and greed - y,__ un - right - eous,__ un - ho - ly.__ Un - do me,__ un - do__ me.__ Ab - ba, Fa - ther, you must won - der__ why__ more times than Pe - ter I__ have__ de - nied.__ Three nails__ and a cross__ to prove__ I owe__

219

THY WORD

**Words and Music by MICHAEL W. SMITH
and AMY GRANT**

Moderately

Thy Word is a lamp_ un-to_ my feet_ and a_

light_ un-to_ my path.

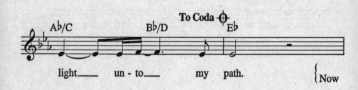

Thy Word is a lamp_ un-to_ my feet_ and a_

light_ un-to_ my path. {Now

When I feel_ a - fraid, think I've lost_ my_ way,
I will not_ for - get Your love for me,_ and_ yet my

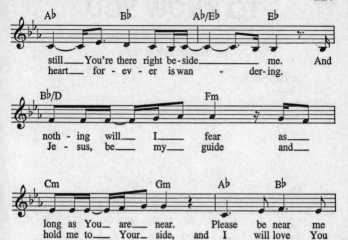

still___ You're there right be-side___ me. And
heart___ for - ev - er is wan - der-ing.

noth - ing will___ I___ fear as___
Je - sus, be___ my___ guide and___

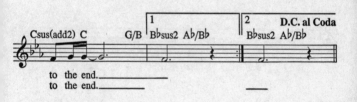

long as You___ are___ near. Please be near me
hold me to___ Your___ side, and I will love You

1 **2** **D.C. al Coda**

to the end.___
to the end.___

CODA

path, and a___ light___ un - to___ my

path. You're the___ light___ un - to___ my path.

TO KNOW YOU

Words and Music by NICHOLE NORDEMAN
and MARK HAMMOND

Moderately slow

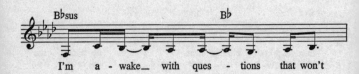

It's well__ past mid - night and

I'm a - wake__ with ques - tions that won't

wait__ for day - light,

sep - a - rat - ing fact__ from my i - mag-

- i - nar - y fic - tion on this

shelf of my___ con - vic - tion. I

need to find___ a place___ where You and I___

___ come face___ to face. Thom - as need-ed
Nic - o - de - mus

proof that You___ had real - ly ris - en
could not un - der - stand___ how You could

un - de - feat - ed.
tru - ly free___ us. He

When he placed___ his fin - gers where the
strug - gled with___ the im - age of a

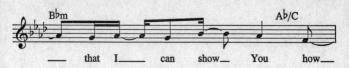

that I___ can show___ You how___

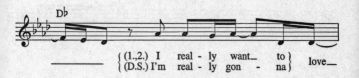

___ { (1.,2.) I real - ly want___ to }
{ (D.S.) I'm real - ly gon - na } love___

___ You.___ Be pa-tient with___ my doubt; I'm just

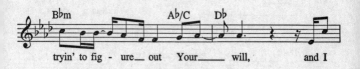

tryin' to fig - ure___ out Your___ will, and I

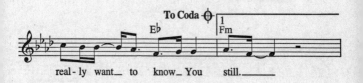

real - ly want___ to know___ You still.___

still.___ No___ more

WE CAN MAKE A DIFFERENCE

Words and Music by MARK HEIMERMANN and DAVID MULLEN

Steady groove

We live in a dream___ if we real-ly think___
Do you know a man___ who's need-ing a hand?___

___ ev-'ry-thing's al - right,___ yeah.
Don't you walk on by,___ oh.

This world is in need,___ cry-ing out to be freed,___
A sis-ter is sad,___ lost all that she had,___

we got-ta shed some light,___ oh.
we got-ta take the time,___ oh.

(1.,D.S.) Teach the world to smile___ and hear an-gels sing,___
(2.) Look a - round your world,___ it will tes - ti - fy.___

feel the breath of God___ and the pow'r_ it brings._
Some have emp - ty hearts,_ some have hun - gry eyes.___

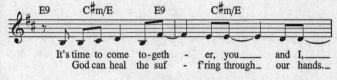

It's time to come to-geth - er, you___ and I,___
God can heal the suf - f'ring through_ our hands.___

To Coda ⊕

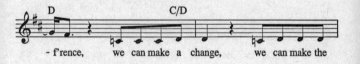

___ and share the love of Je - sus Christ.⎫
_____ Find com-pas-sion, take___ a stand.⎬ We can make a dif-

- f'rence, we can make a change, we can make the

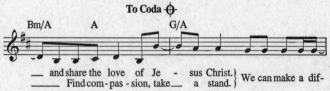

world a bet - ter place._____ We can make a dif-

- f'rence, we can make a____change, we can make the

230

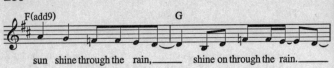

sun shine through the rain,_____ shine on through the rain._____

— Do do doot do do,_____ do do doot do do,_

— do do doot do doot do do._____

Do do doot do do,_____ do do doot do do,_

— do do doot do doot do do._____

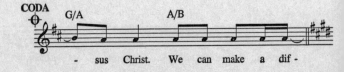

- sus Christ. We can make a dif -

WE NEED JESUS

By JOHN ELEFANTE,
DINO ELEFANTE and SCOTT SPRINGER

When will the world see that we_ need Je - sus?

If we o - pen_ our_ eyes, we will
When our hearts are_ as_ one and be -

all re - al - ize that He loves us._

lieve that He's_ the Son of our God._

The Lord is our God, and we shall nev - er

want. The Lord is our God, and

Will we ev-er un-der-stand Je-sus

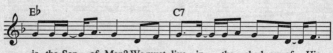

is the Son_ of Man? We must live in_ the_ shad-ow of_ His

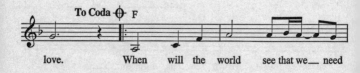

love. When will the world see that we_ need

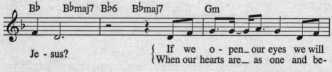

Je - sus? { If we o - pen our eyes we will
{ When our hearts are_ as one and be-

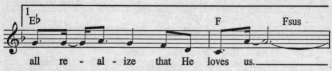

all re - al - ize that He loves us._

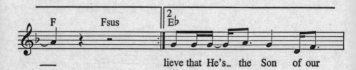

_ lieve that He's_ the Son of our

God._

WHEN IT'S TIME TO GO

Words and Music by JEFF SILVEY
and BILLY SIMON

Moderately, in 2

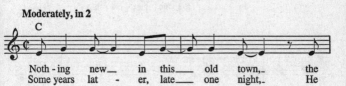

Noth - ing new__ in this__ old town,__ the
Some years lat - er, late__ one night,__ He

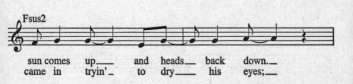

sun comes up__ and heads__ back down.__
came in tryin'__ to dry__ his eyes;__

Work - ing hard__ from dawn__ to dusk__ a - gain.
He re - al - ized what He__ was born__ to do.__

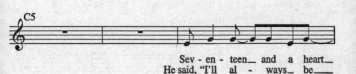

Sev - en - teen__ and a heart__
He said, "I'll al - ways__ be__

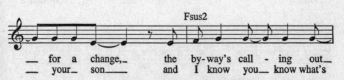

__ for a change,__ the by-way's call - ing out__
__ your__ son and I know you__ know what's

B♭sus2

_ His_ name,_ but not_ yet;_ there's
go - in'_ on._ It's the hard - est thing to

F/A   F   C5

too much go - in' on._ 'Cause
think of leav - in' you._ But

G   F

dad - dy needs_ a hand and ma - ma's
this world needs_ a hand and I've_ got

G   F   G

ten - der heart_ might crum - ble to_ the
just the thing_ they need to make_ it

Am   G

ground. Though they'd un - der- stand,_ He
through. It's so clear to me,_ though I

C

felt like say - ing, } "When it's time_ to go,_ you've got_ to
know what's com- ing. }

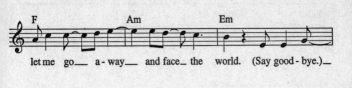

let me go— a-way— and face— the world. (Say good-bye.)—

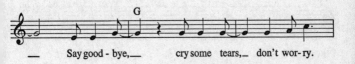

— Say good-bye,— cry some tears,— don't wor-ry.

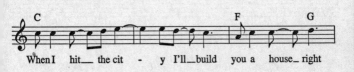

When I hit— the cit - y I'll—build you a house— right

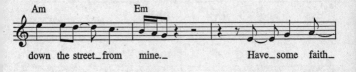

down the street— from mine.— Have— some faith—

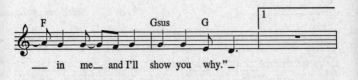

— in me— and I'll show you why."—

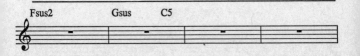

Say good - bye,— cry some tears,— don't wor-ry.

When I hit— the cit - y I'll— build you a house— right

down the street— from mine.— Oh,—

— have— some faith— in me— and I'll

1, 2

show you why."—

3

show you why."—

(Instrumental)

WHERE THERE IS FAITH

Words and Music by
BILLY SIMON

I be - lieve___ in faith - ful - ness,
There's a man___ a - cross_ the sea,

___ I be - lieve___ in giv - ing of___
___ nev - er heard___ the sound_ of free -

___ my - self___ for some - one___
- dom ring,___ on - ly___ in

else.___ I be - lieve
his dreams.___ There's a la -

___ in peace___ and love,___ I be - lieve___
- dy dressed___ in black___ in a mo -

243

WISDOM

Words and Music by
TWILA PARIS

Moderately slow groove

I see a mul - ti - tude_ of peo - ple,
There is a mo - ment of_ de - ci - sion,

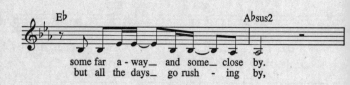

some far a - way_ and some_ close by.
but all the days_ go rush - ing by,

They weave to - geth - er new re - li -
an un - der - cur - rent of con - fu -

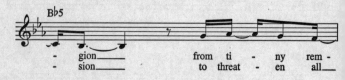

- gion_ from ti - ny rem -
- sion_ to threat - en all

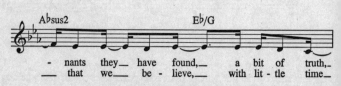

- nants they_ have found,_ a bit of truth,_
_ that we_ be - lieve,_ with lit - tle time

— a great - er lie.___
— to won - der why.___

And all the proph - ets stand__ and sing__
And all the proph - ets sing__ the same__

— a pleas - ant song,___
— fa - mil - iar song;___

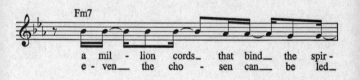

a mil - lion cords__ that bind__ the spir -
e - ven__ the cho - sen can__ be led__

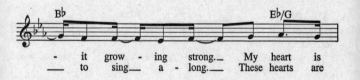

- it grow - ing strong.__ My heart is
__ to sing__ a - long.__ These hearts are

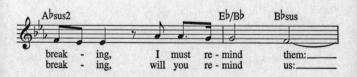

break - ing, I must re - mind them:___
break - ing, will you re - mind us:___

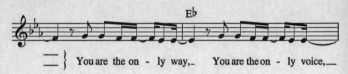

You are the on - ly way,__ You are the on - ly voice,__

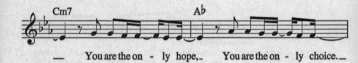

__ You are the on - ly hope,__ You are the on - ly choice.__

__ You are the one__ true God,__ no mat-ter what__ we say.__

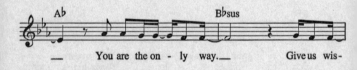

__ You are the breath__ of life,__

__ You are the on - ly way.__ Give us wis-

- dom.__ Give us wis-

- dom.___

You choose the sim - ple things___ to

o - ver - come___ the wise.___

Wis - dom___ is grant - ed in the name___ of Je - sus

Christ,_____ in the name___ of Je - sus

Christ._____ You are the on - ly way,___

___ You are the on - ly voice,___

248

YOU ARE THE ANSWER

Words and Music by MATT HUESMANN
and REGIE HAMM

250

I hear_ the voic - es,_ the souls in need_ of You,_
mes - sage_ of hope that_ can on - ly be found in You,_

'cause)
'cause)   You are_ the an -

- swer   and the mean - ing of life

to hearts_ in dark - ness, and the source of the light.

As we walk this hu - man road,_ ev - 'ry

ques - tion will find You are the an - swer.___

A - cross the

GUITAR CHORD FRAMES

	C	Cm	C+	C6	Cm6

C

	C#	C#m	C#+	C#6	C#m6

C♯/D♭

	D	Dm	D+	D6	Dm6

D

	E♭	E♭m	E♭+	E♭6	E♭m6

E♭/D♯

	E	Em	E+	E6	Em6

E

	F	Fm	F+	F6	Fm6

F

This guitar chord reference includes 120 commonly used chords. For a more complete guide to guitar chords, see "THE PAPERBACK CHORD BOOK" (HL00702009).

C	C7	Cmaj7	Cm7	C7sus	Cdim7
C#/Db	C#7	C#maj7	C#m7	C#7sus	C#dim7
D	D7	Dmaj7	Dm7	D7sus	Ddim7
Eb/D#	Eb7	Ebmaj7	Ebm7	Eb7sus	Ebdim7
E	E7	Emaj7	Em7	E7sus	Edim7
F	F7	Fmaj7	Fm7	F7sus	Fdim7

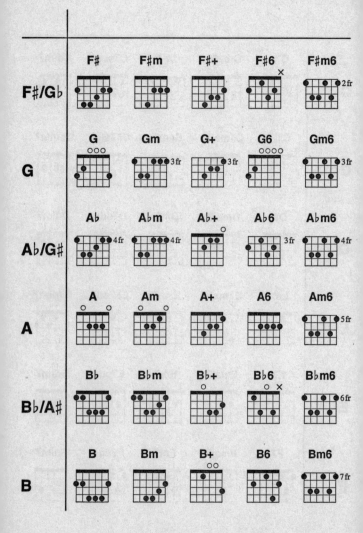